This library edition published in 2013 by Walter Foster Publishing, Inc.
Walter Foster Library
3 Wrigley, Suite A
Irvine, CA 92618

Printed in Mankato, Minnesota, USA by CG Book Printers, a division of Corporate Graphics.

First Library Edition

Library of Congress Cataloging-in-Publication Data

Keely, Jack.
  [Starting out in cartooning]
  Cartooning 1 / by Jack Keely ; with Carson Van Osten.
      pages cm. -- (How to draw & paint)
  Includes bibliographical references and index.
1. Cartooning--Technique. I. Osten, Carson van. II. Title.
  NC1320.K43 2013
  741.5'1--dc23
                                                          2013012506

052013
18134

9 8 7 6 5 4 3 2 1

Cartooning 1

Cartoons can charm. They can make you laugh. They can tell thrilling tales. And often, they do all three at the same time. What comes to mind when you think of cartooning? Comic strips and cartoons are only a few of the venues open to cartoonists. Cartoons also adorn and populate greeting cards, children's books, and advertisements. All you need to get started are a few books, some basic techniques, and a little imagination. In this book I will show you how you can create your own private universe and bring to life anything from a talking dog to a mutant from Mars. As you start on your way, you will be amazed at how easy it is to develop your own cartoon characters. — *Jack Keely*.

CONTENTS

Getting Started

YOU DON'T NEED MUCH to get started in this racket. One famous cartoon character began his career as a doodle made with a felt-tip marker on a napkin. However, a few basic supplies will make life a lot easier for the budding cartoonist.

The Basics

For starters, you'll need a pencil for rough sketches, an eraser, some paper to draw on, and a pen or marker to ink in your final drawings. Which pencil? What kind of paper? Don't get stressed out worrying about what supplies to select. This isn't brain surgery or rocket science, and it doesn't really matter. It just depends on what you like to work with. That's right. You've got the ball, but here are a few general tips to steer you through the sea of supplies.

▶ **ERASER** Fat, pink erasers like the ones on the ends of pencils leave crumbs all over the place. You'll need a kneaded eraser. It doesn't leave crumbs, and you can shape it into a point to get into small areas. You can also stretch it, squash it, and squeeze it into funny shapes while you're waiting for inspiration to strike.

▲ **DRAWING PENCIL** Pencils have different degrees of hardness. H pencils have hard leads, and B pencils have soft ones. An HB is somewhere in the middle, with a lead that is hard enough to keep a point and soft enough to shade with, making it a good pencil for sketching. Want more drama? 2B or 3B pencils have softer leads that allow you to make stronger lines. I suggest you use an HB pencil to sketch in guidelines and work out details on your cartoons.

▲ **DIP PEN** I sometimes use an old-fashioned crow-quill pen with black India ink to make my cartoons extra expressive. These funky-looking pens come with many different nibs—from very fine tips to broad-edged, chisel points. (I recommend that you start off with a medium-point pen because it's the easiest one to use and the most versatile.) Dip just the point in the ink. Don't drown the pen. As you increase and decrease pressure on the pen, your line will become thicker and thinner. It takes time to master this pen, so start with some loose sketches.

Think Ink

Once you have perfected your drawing in pencil, you will want to ink it so that it will have rich, black lines. You have a lot of options depending on what type of line you are after, from ordinary felt-tip markers to crow-quill pens, fountain pens, and technical pens. Many cartoonists prefer a pen or a brush and black drawing ink. Try a variety of different inking tools, and see which ones you like best.

▶ **BRUSH** The fluid lines of a brush and black ink can be delicate and precise or boldly dramatic, depending on the amount of pressure you use. A brush is also good for filling in large areas of black. Buy a good-quality brush at an art store. Cheap brushes won't keep a point and won't give you an eloquent line.

▶ **TECHNICAL PEN** A technical pen offers you a lot of control. These pens come in a wide variety of points, enabling you to vary your line widths. The lines created are consistently even and precise, although they may look somewhat mechanical, without much "flair." Mechanical pens are fun to use if you like to do a lot of minute crosshatching or stippling.

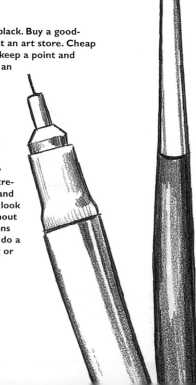

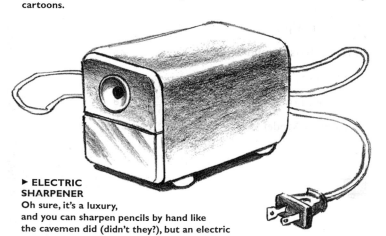

▶ **ELECTRIC SHARPENER** Oh sure, it's a luxury, and you can sharpen pencils by hand like the cavemen did (didn't they?), but an electric one gives you a great point and makes a satisfying noise. Ask Santa.

Study Up!

The better video stores are packed with great samples of animation that will help you get your creative juices flowing. Check out some interesting experimental animation and some of the groundbreaking cartoons from the past—not just the latest hits.

Did you know that every second you watch, there are 24 individual drawings that go by? Try making a few sketches of some frames.

Artist's Tip

Try using the pause button to stop at interesting poses, gestures, and compositions. Make a sketch of what you like.

Extra, Extra!

As you progress, you'll find your collection of art supplies growing. You'll want an adjustable lamp to shed some light on your subject. And you'll be cutting up a lot of paper, so a good pair of scissors or an artist's razor knife are essential. Don't forget a drafting brush to whisk away eraser crumbs and other debris from your masterpiece—and a T-square and a couple of triangles will be invaluable if you decide to start laying out your own comic strips. Finally, drafting tape will hold your drawing securely in place on your desk or drafting board.

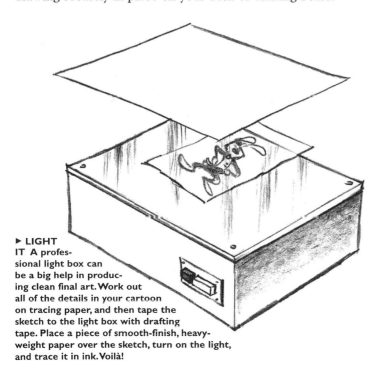

▶ **LIGHT IT** A professional light box can be a big help in producing clean final art. Work out all of the details in your cartoon on tracing paper, and then tape the sketch to the light box with drafting tape. **Place a piece of smooth-finish, heavy-weight paper over the sketch, turn on the light, and trace it in ink. Voilà!**

Paper Training

Play around with different types of paper and drawing surfaces, and find out what suits you. Papers and illustration boards come with smooth surfaces and rough ones. The texture of the surface will affect the kinds of lines you can produce. You'll need a smooth surface for precise, clean lines, but rough paper may suit you if you're after a textured, arty effect. For generating a lot of ideas fast, the nice, smooth surface of white bond typing paper is great. To finesse a cartoon character, I like to use tracing paper. I sketch out a drawing, then slip it under another sheet of tracing paper and try it again. I'll change the expression, make the nose bigger, switch the pose around, or add a hat. I keep mucking around this way and that until it's just the way I want it.

TRACING HEAVY WEIGHT 9 X 12"

▶ **TRACE IT**
If you prefer working on tracing paper but want your final cartoon to be on a thick paper stock, here's how you do it: First ink over your masterpiece on tracing paper, and then photocopy it onto card stock. You can even color it in with felt-tip markers for some additional pizzazz!

Create a Collection of References

As you go along, begin to establish your own reference library. In addition to books on cartooning, animation, and illustration, you'll find inspiration in clip art books, comic books, and humor magazines. A morgue, or clipping file, is also helpful. If you see a photo that might make a good reference or a cartoon card that makes you laugh, save it to spark your imagination on some rainy day.

Which Way?

THERE'S MORE THAN ONE ROUTE to Cartoon Town. Remember, this is an art, not a science, and you can make up a lot of your own rules. Don't be afraid to break out of the mold. Cartoons can be cute, cuddly, wacky, weird, thrilling, or chilling, depending on who's steering the pen. And in an arena where bugs wear clothes, mild-mannered reporters moonlight as superheroes, and teapots talk, anything goes.

But hey, you have to start somewhere. In this book, you'll see three different approaches— three sets of guidelines for creating different types of cartoons. I've also thrown in a few extra tidbits of information, and a few examples of a graphic kind of cartooning. Try the different styles on for size and see which one fits you best. As you continue to draw and create cartoon characters, you'll develop a style that's unique to you.

SUZY
by ANN SNOWE

◄ **TOO CUTE FOR WORDS** Kids identify and parents chuckle knowingly at the mischievous antics of cartoon small fry, which makes them popular styles for picture books and cards.

Artist's Tip
The guidelines in this book can help you chart your own unique course. But remember, every rule can be broken!

Cute Cartoons
A lot of comic strips, children's books, and greeting cards are populated by precocious, big-eyed moppets and their lovable furry friends. These characters are endlessly produced as collectible figurines and ornaments as well. There's nothing like a little kid or a puppy to bring out warm and fuzzy feelings in even the grumpiest reader.

▼ **TOTALLY WILD AND WACKY** The hero may be a caveman, a robot, or a talking pig, but you can be certain he'll be put through the wringer before the curtain comes down on the cartoon or comic strip action.

Zany Cartoons

The wild characters and slapstick humor of zany cartoons are a warped reflection of our world. The situations the characters find themselves in are often familiar to us (late for work, annoyed by a neighbor, or baby-sitting a brat, for instance), and their ridiculous responses are wildly exaggerated versions of our own.

STOP! STOP! BAD DOG!

CRASH!

?

Realistic Cartoons

Comic books are bursting with tales of heroism and derring-do. For these bold adventures, a more realistic style of drawing is called for. Cartoon realism isn't exactly realistic. Everything is stylized and stripped of extraneous details for maximum impact.

MUTT

THE NEW ADVENTURE!

◄ **TRUE TO LIFE** Realistic cartoons display a knowledge of anatomy and perspective presented in a stylized version where everything is simplified. This particular art style is often employed in advertisements and editorial cartoons as well.

The Cute Crew

THE CUTIES IN THESE CARTOONS often have infant proportions—big heads; small, pear-shaped bodies; and chubby arms and legs. The faces are wide-eyed with high foreheads, and somewhat shy in appearance, and the nose is always small. Cute characters often have swayed backs, protruding tummies and fannies, and almost no neck—if they have one at all! Tiny feet look cute on kids, and oversized paws make a kitten or puppy adorable. Look at the common characteristics in the cartoons on these pages, and notice how "round" they appear. Overall, they charm us with their innocence.

◀ **BABY FACE** The basic formula for designing a cute expression is to locate the eyes, ears, nose, and mouth in the lower half of the face. Also, make the eyes large, round, and trusting, and space them wide apart.

Artist's Tip
A graphic, stylized cartoon technique works well for advertising and trademarks, where you need a fast read and won't need to create a lot of varying emotions.

▶ **CURIOUSER AND CURIOUSER** The little nature lover below has his hands resting on his knees in a childlike manner as he bends over to greet a new friend.

▲ **SIZE COUNTS** Cartoon characters are measured in heads. Cute characters' heads are very large in proportion to their bodies. The little tykes above were drawn three heads high.

◀ **ENCHANTING EXTRAS** This is a pencil sketch in which I started out rough and recopied with tracing paper several times until I arrived at the finished drawing. Notice how the tip of the tongue sticking out adds to the "cute" quotient.

Bright Eyes

Little kids' eyes are large in relation to their faces. Cartoonists capitalize on this fact, and it's standard practice to draw innocent characters with big, round peepers. Large, round eyes "read" well on the page because they are very expressive. You can create a variety of expressions by rotating the irises from side to side or raising and lowering the eyelid.

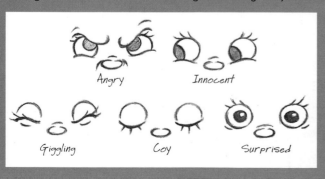

Angry   Innocent

Giggling   Coy   Surprised

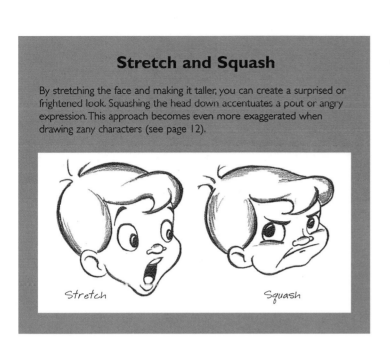

Stretch and Squash

By stretching the face and making it taller, you can create a surprised or frightened look. Squashing the head down accentuates a pout or angry expression. This approach becomes even more exaggerated when drawing zany characters (see page 12).

Stretch   *Squash*

Cute Expressions

The faces of the cuties can display a wide range of emotion. A few lines can quickly render a cranky pout, a look of wide-eyed wonder, or a happy grin. But don't overdo the details! Deeply furrowed brows and gnashing teeth are inappropriate here. It's simplicity that gives these babes their charm.

IMAGINATIVE CHARACTERS The cute approach often works well for fantasy cartoons. Just adding a set of wings or a pair of baby-sized, pointed ears can quickly transform the kid next door into an angel, a leprechaun, fairy, or elf.

▶ SIMPLY CHARMING This ice cream lover shows a more stylized method of drawing a cute character. She has also been drawn with more extreme proportions— the head is as big as the body, and giving her an oversized hand draws attention to the enormous ice-cream cone. Her facial features, hair, and clothing are simple and graphic, making her as cute as pie.

◀ WHO'S GOT THE BUTTON? This curious cutie has small, button eyes, which can be very effective for creating a cute expression in a simple, graphic-style drawing like this.

▲ PLAYTIME Little kids shouldn't look as stiff as Wall Street bankers. Children twist, squirm, jump, and gyrate. Expressive body language helps tell the story. Sailor Sally's outstretched hands make it clear that she's just sent her sailboat on its maiden voyage.

Warm and Fuzzy

THESE HUGGABLE BUNDLES of fur and feathers follow the same guidelines as those for cute children. Cute cartoon animals are often slightly *anthropomorphized,* meaning they've been given certain human characteristics. Often the dark button eyes of animals are replaced with human-style eyes and eyelashes, and, occasionally, eyebrows. In addition, their mouths are frequently curved into an appealing smile. These cute critters are just begging to be picked up and petted.

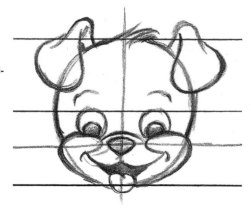

▶ **PUTTING IT IN PROPORTION** The design of the cute animal face is the same as the one for the cute kid face. Locate the eyes, nose, and mouth in the lower half. The eyes are large and round. Chubby cheeks overlap the eyes.

Small Wonders

The basic cute construction is a combination of circles, ovals, and rounded "friendly" shapes. (Save sharp angles for a wicked witch!) As you can see here, almost any animal you can think of can be cute and friendly when drawn with this design formula. Then put it in action. The little animals on these pages are animated and lively, reflecting the actions of real baby animals. Making quick sketches from life of your own pets, zoo animals, or squirrels in the park will help you get a feeling for how animals move.

▲ **CREATING A FULL FIGURE** To construct a cute little animal, such as the pup, start with a body shaped like a plump bean. Add a circle for the head that has just about the same volume as the body.

◀ **NOTHING TO BE AFRAID OF** Tiny creatures with bright eyes and paws like hands, mice are among the most appealing cartoon animals.

▶ **THE LOOK** This wise quacker gives an engaging, sidelong glance.

◀ **BODY LANGUAGE** This cuddly bunny looks up, emphasizing her small size and fragility. The tilt of the head and the springy stance add to the appeal.

▶ **BEGGING TO BE LOVED** The wagging tail and little tongue make this smiling pup look even happier.

▶ **PLAYFUL AS A KITTEN** Notice the childlike proportions of this adorable kitten. The huge eyes give it an innocent expression.

◀ **REAL DETAILS** The turtle's wrinkled knees and beaky face are realistic details that make this slowpoke believable.

▶ VARIATIONS ON A THEME
Bunnies, squirrels, and chipmunks are drawn following the same formula, but bunnies have slightly larger cheeks and narrower foreheads. A bunny's eyes are set a little higher but they still rest on the cheeks. A little suggestion of oversized front teeth adds to this character's appeal.

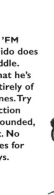

▶ MAKE 'EM MOVE Fido does a dog paddle. Notice that he's made entirely of curved lines. Try to give action poses a rounded, fluid look. No hard edges for these guys.

Artist's Tip
When drawing "cute" characters, keep the shading and details to a minimum.

▶ THE CUTE TREATMENT Fido's finny friends have been "cutified" with human eyes and chubby cheeks. The rounded lips are suitably fishy without sacrificing a smile.

About Face

You can start with a simple, ball-shaped head and spin off in many directions. Here we've started with a babyish head and a pair of round eyes and created a variety of cute animals by changing the ears, nose, and mouth. Add a tuft of hair, eyelashes, or maybe some whiskers to finish your cartoon animal.

Start with a basic head shape based on a circle with chubby cheeks.

Down-turned eyebrows and mouth let you know this pup's in a cranky mood.

A softer jaw line, plumper cheeks, and rounder nose are appropriate for a pig.

The kitten's mouth points up in the center, and its little nose points down.

The Human Touch

GIVING ANIMALS HUMAN CHARACTERISTICS (called *anthropomorphism*) allows us to use cute animals as stand-ins for people. These characters often wear clothes, drive cars, and live in houses. Their bodies becomes more human in proportion and yet retain some degree of animal identity. These animal kids are among the most popular cartoon characters.

► **CONSTRUCTING HANDS** To give your cute animals human-like hands, start with a simple circle for the palm, and then draw three or four short, fat fingers.

◄ **KID PROPORTIONS** Cute animal-people can be drawn with the same proportions as cute kids; both kittens here are 2-1/2 heads high. However, you don't always have to use the same drawing style to make your characters look young and cute. Here I've drawn the first kitten with button-eyed, graphic simplicity and I've given the second saucer-shaped eyes and a wide, white muzzle.

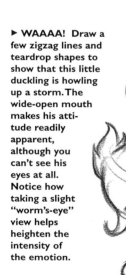

► **WAAAA!** Draw a few zigzag lines and teardrop shapes to show that this little duckling is howling up a storm. The wide-open mouth makes his attitude readily apparent, although you can't see his eyes at all. Notice how taking a slight "worm's-eye" view helps heighten the intensity of the emotion.

Cute as a Bug in a Rug

Insects are perennially popular cartoon creatures, and they pose unique design problems. How many legs do you draw? Do you give smiles and noses to bugs? What is the fashionable insect wearing this season? Stripes and polka dots are always "in," but it's up to you, pal.

Our bee's a real honey. His big head and bug eyes follow the cute kid formula, but his body shape makes him suitably buggy. The demure ladybug's wings become a jacket, her cuff and hemline showing beneath. Her curlicue antennae are as feminine as a spit curl.

Hands Down

On animal-people, paws become three- or four-fingered hands—small, pudgy, and cute. Keep the fingers short. For birds, make the feather fingers more tapered. Horses, pigs, and other animals with hooves present a challenge. You can draw hooves as gloved hands. Or draw them to look like hooves, but more flexible, like a hand inside a sock or mitten.

Typecasting

From the brave lion to the sly fox, animals have been used to embody human traits in stories from Aesop's fables to the Saturday morning cartoons. You can effectively employ these stereotypes to allow people some immediate understanding of your character's personality. It's no surprise that the little owl to the right has his beak in a book, as everyone knows owls are wise. You can also get mileage out of turning stereotypes upside down by drawing a fearless mouse or a speedy turtle.

▲ **BEAR FOOTED** Whether pigeon-toed and knock-kneed or impatiently tapping a foot, these bears do not stand on formality. Giving your bears bare feet is a cute alternative to drawing shoes—plus it makes the little guys seem vulnerable.

Focus on Feet

Keep the poses of your animal kids lively and energetic—even if they're standing still. Giving youngsters a toe-in or toe-out stance is appealing and keeps them from looking stiff and grown-up. Also, to avoid making bare feet look too humanlike, keep the number of toes to three or four—and skip the toenails!

Artist's Tip
Details such as long ears and fluffy tails help identify an animal in people's clothing.

◄ **HAPPY HOPPER** Bunny boy is drawn with kidlike proportions, outfit, and pose, but his padded feet remind you that he's really a rabbit in boy's clothing.

◄ **SHOE-IN** Animal kids (or should I say, "kittens"?) sometimes wear shoes. Keep them simple, like the ones shown here. A lot of fussy detail with laces, heels, and so on is distracting.

Zany Is as Zany Does

ZANY DRAWING IS THE EXTREME SPORT of cartooning. The zany character's mission is to look funny and do funny things. Everything about him is excessive. When he's scared, make him jump out of his skin—literally. Or make him melt into a puddle on a scorching hot day. He may be a loudmouth or a shrinking violet, a villain or a do-gooder. The zany character lives on the edge with life's volume at full blast, and he is usually one sandwich short of a picnic.

◄ HELLO! Meet the typical, upstanding cartoon zany. He's a humanized animal with a pear-shaped body. He might be a dog, but I'm not really sure. Floppy ears would definitely make him canine. You could also change him into a fox by adding pointy ears and a full fluffy tail. A good basic zany like this can be customized in any direction you wish.

▲ A HANDY GUY Our hero's arms and legs are like rubber hoses, and they can stretch for extreme action. Immense hands and feet render him clumsy and clownish, and white gloves make his hands stand out even more. Four-fingered hands are easier to draw than ones with five digits, they allow for a full range of motion, and they look funny to boot.

Zany Expressions

This loudmouth was drawn with an undersized cranium to show that it holds a small, if mischievous, mind. The lower part of his face is wide to accommodate a big mouth and a bulbous nose. His eyes are close together with beady pupils and eyelids that fly up in astonishment and scrunch down in anger. Facial elasticity is the key since tremendous, rubbery features broadcast emotions quickly.

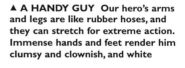

Surprised

Amused

Angry

Sad

Glowering

Sleepy

Sheepish

Going Together

Think out the logic behind your animal zanies. Are they all jungle animals or farmyard friends? It usually doesn't make sense to mix humans and dressed-up animals unless you have a reason—a bear family versus a hunter, for example. However, that rule—like all the other rules concerning cartoons—can be broken if you do so intentionally and not by accident.

STRETCHING IT Enormous google eyes, teardrop-shaped bodies, and goofy attitudes are among the elements that link this doofus dog and cat couple.

▲ **GROUPING 'EM** Give your gang a consistent look. These characters have individual personalities, but since they're designed with a pear-shaped head and simple, rounded features, they work well as a group.

Artist's Tip
Remember big versus small. The fast-talking bird below wouldn't be nearly as effective if he were as big as the bulldog.

Animal Wisecrackers

Zany cartoons offer another golden opportunity for anthropomorphism (see pages 8 and 10). If your character's a cop with hanging jowls like a bulldog, why not make him a real bulldog? If a tyrant is a bit of a pig, make him a real pig! A cow is a pretty funny-looking animal—so a cow in a cocktail dress can be even funnier.

▶ **BIG BULLY** The thuggish features of a big bulldog make for an ideal bully. Putting him in a uniform can be even funnier. The size relationships among characters can accent the action. Here the imposing stature of the cop makes his pugnacious stance even more intimidating to the poor little birdbrain.

13

Crazy Characters

SPEND AN HOUR ON A PARK BENCH and watch the passing parade with a sketchbook. Bespectacled computer nerds, bleached blondes teetering on stiletto heels, red-faced brats, and business-suited blimps will quickly fill your pages. By emphasizing the characteristics your fellow humans display, you'll find that you have a wealth of satiric material to work with. Exaggeration and simplification are the keys. A receding hairline becomes a shiny dome, dreamy eyes are as large as saucers, and a smattering of freckles becomes five or six polka dots.

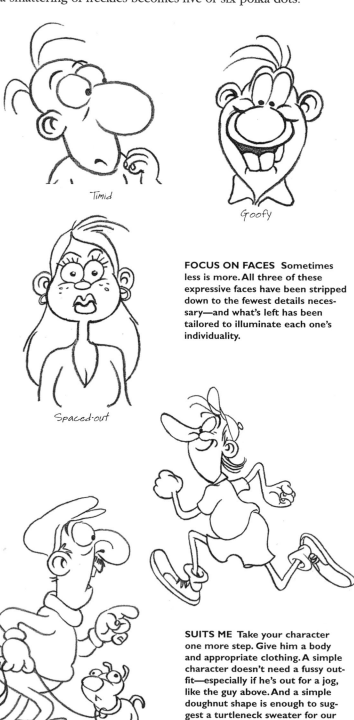

Timid

Goofy

FOCUS ON FACES Sometimes less is more. All three of these expressive faces have been stripped down to the fewest details necessary—and what's left has been tailored to illuminate each one's individuality.

Spaced-out

SUITS ME Take your character one more step. Give him a body and appropriate clothing. A simple character doesn't need a fussy outfit—especially if he's out for a jog, like the guy above. And a simple doughnut shape is enough to suggest a turtleneck sweater for our dog lover. All you need is the silhouette of a heel to give the impression of trousers and shoes without drawing them at all!

The Nose Knows

Here's a good way to spark some ideas. Quickly sketch a variety of possible cartoon head shapes. Pear and sausage shapes make good skulls for cartoon zanies. Then stick a wacky nose on each of the heads. For some reason, all the funny nose shapes start with the letter "B"—bean, ball, balloon, and banana! Now, what comes to mind? A warty witch? A silly sailor?

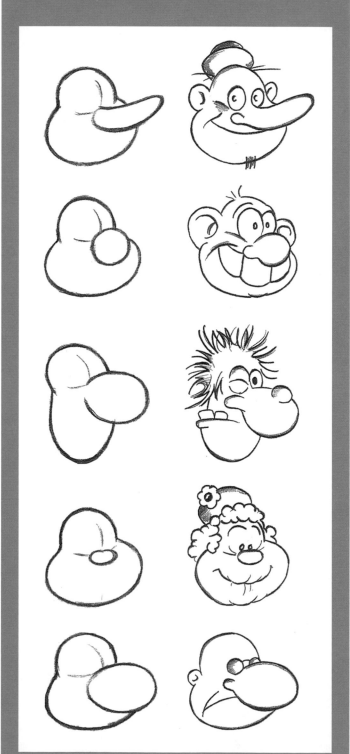

▶ **SCARY PAIR** The "nagging wife" provides a perfect opportunity for exaggeration in a cartoon. The extreme angle of Screaming Mimi's body combined with her contorted face gives added force to her foghorn yell. Long locks, scraggly beard, and hairy arms give beefy Biker Bob the requisite woolly-boolly look.

Getting a Graphic Start

These drawings have been created using as few lines as possible. Notice what is missing in these drawings. Insignificant details have been omitted. Positive and negative areas can be used to great effect in black and white cartoons. The dark shape of a vest or jacket gives weight and anchors the drawing. This can be particularly effective when contrasted with a thin, whimsical line.

GO PICASSO The design of comic characters can be influenced by abstract art. Why not put both eyes on the same side of the head? Have the nose face east and the toes face west. Feel free to be as wacky as you "wanna" be.

Critter Crazy

ONE TRICK FOR DRAWING CARTOON ANIMALS is to think of them as an assembly of simple shapes, like globes, sausages, pears, and eggs. By playing off the natural colors and markings of your animal characters, you can have critters who are spotted, striped, and wildly colored, adding to the visual excitement. Animals work well in zany cartoons. The dog-chasing-cat-chasing-mouse scenario has had a lot of mileage, but there's always a fresh approach to familiar material. And the array of animals as potential subject matter ranges from Aunt Biddy's parakeet to the abominable snowman.

Exaggerate!

The bulldog wildly barking at a mailman out of reach or the hairy ape mimicking human behavior provide ample opportunity for the kind of squashed and stretched facial expressions and slapstick antics that are the basis of zany cartoon humor. Lumpish camels, fat pigs, and contented cows have funny faces and peculiar body shapes that give you plenty of material to work with.

◄ **HOLD THE BACON** You can create all kinds of funny animals with sausage, egg, and muffin shapes.

► **WELL DONE** Put together a short, fat, sausage body, a few head-and-hump egg shapes, and some muffin hooves and suddenly you've got yourself a camel.

► **HORSING AROUND** Start with a sausage body (or is it a pinto bean?) and two eggs for a head.

► **GIDDYUP** Now add balls for joints at the knees and ankles and four muffin hooves.

◄ **FUNNY FEATHERS** The contrast of a fat egg body and long, hose-like legs make the ostrich an appealing zany. Not much skull space is needed to house his birdbrain.

◄ **HORSE LAUGH** Finally, sketch in the ears, eyes, and smile. The details such as saddle, lasso, and bridle are carefully delineated. But notice that they are composed of clean simple shapes. Saddle up!

Rubber Legs

The animals on this page all share a sausage body and have long hoses for legs. Their rubbery limbs make them look flexible, fluid, and funny. Big clodhopper feet add to the clumsily comic effect. Try this approach with other agile, long-limbed animals such as monkeys, cows, and giraffes.

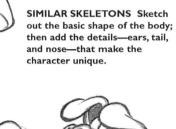

SIMILAR SKELETONS Sketch out the basic shape of the body; then add the details—ears, tail, and nose—that make the character unique.

► **FLAP-JAWED** Big-nosed, dreamy Fido is a jowly, drooling good ol' boy. His floppy ears and outsized collar accentuate the goofiness of this harmless clown.

◄ **TRÉS CHIC** Fido and Fifi share the same canine construction used to very different effects. Flirty, long-lashed eyes, a pert, pointed nose, and soft lines combine to make this poodle fetching and feminine, though still funny. On her, a dog collar becomes a chic necklace.

GRRRR! When Leo roars, his head angles back and stretches out to display his fearsome teeth, and his eyes screw up into a squinty line. The bulbous nose, big feet, and curvy, soft form of this king of beasts makes him appear silly and harmless in spite of his claws and sharp teeth.

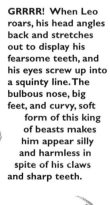

Get Real!

SUPERHERO STORIES, SCIENCE FICTION and fantasy tales combine elements of reality with humor and make-believe. A somewhat more realistic approach is often called for to make these yarns seem plausible. This is a little bit more complicated than other types of cartooning, because basic knowledge of anatomy and perspective is required. Some practice at life drawing can come in very handy.

Head Start

A good way to get started in this arena is by drawing faces—handsome faces, evil faces, scared faces, happy faces. Faces are a lot of fun to draw, and it's important to do them well, as cartooning relies heavily on closeups. Try using a photograph for reference. Study it for the basic pose, and trace or copy it. Animators often make a live action film, project each frame onto paper, and make a rough tracing. This is called roto-scoping. Simplify and stylize your photographic image to develop a cartoon character.

Artist's Tip
When drawing a caricature, use a photo that shows your subject at close range. This way, you can see what features to feature.

▶ **AN EYE FOR AN EYE** Think of the eye as a ball that has a lid above and a pouch below. You see only part of it—never the full circle at one time. And with an icy stare, a startled look, or a sultry glance, the eyes can be a barometer of emotion. What you reveal depends on the shape of the lid and the arch of the brow.

▲ **TRICK-OR-TREAT** To draw this Halloween prankster in a pumpkin patch, I started with a formal shot of soccer-playin' Justin. I copied his arm holding the ball, then flopped it, morphing the soccer balls into pumpkins. Next I enlarged his features, changed his facial expression, and added a mask—and suddenly it's October!

It's a Snap

Cartoonists and illustrators often use photographs for reference, although often the final illustration looks very little like the reference photo. In fact, it probably shouldn't. The photo is just a point of departure. Photos can be a big help if you are trying to draw an eggbeater, a rhinoceros, or a tank, and you don't happen to have one handy. Or you may have to draw someone pitching a baseball, or screaming in horror, and find it hard to visualize. If so, a photograph can help you get the pose or expression right.

▲ **TROPIC FEVER** I drew Katie in Kauai using a standard school photo to base the pose on. Then I elongated her neck and enlarged and stylized (simplified) her facial features. Finally, I added the tropical blooms as well as the suggestion of a breeze in her hair. Aloha!

Making Headway

Skulls are almost always about the same shape in real life. In cartoons, you can start out with a naturalistic oval as a guideline for drawing the head, or feel free to play with any other shape that strikes your fancy.

RECTANGLE Handsome Hank's head is a modified rectangle. I emphasized the strong jawline to give him a rugged look.

KIDNEY BEAN A pointy bean-shape serves as a start for sour Uncle Otto. The downward curves accentuate his dour demeanor.

OVAL Barbara Bombshell started out as a soft oval. When drawing women, keep the shapes rounded and elastic.

Face Off

Faces offer endless variety for the cartoonist. They can be angular and deeply furrowed or as round and soft as a water balloon. Eyes can be wide with wonder or narrowed in suspicion. A nose can be a baby button or strongly arched with flaring nostrils. Does your character deserve full lips or a mouth tightened into a thin line? The faces on this page suggest a variety of personalities. Is the harmless-looking old man a charming grandpa, or does his smile hide an evil secret? Does our villainess have no redeeming qualities—or was she unjustly wronged and now carries a grudge? That's the fun of melodrama!

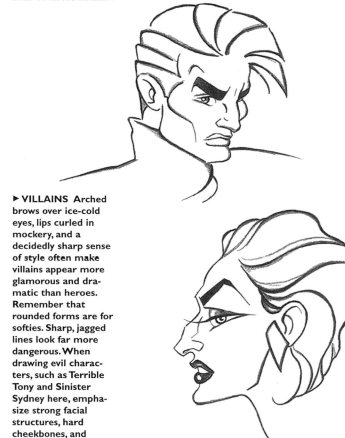

▶ VILLAINS Arched brows over ice-cold eyes, lips curled in mockery, and a decidedly sharp sense of style often make villains appear more glamorous and dramatic than heroes. Remember that rounded forms are for softies. Sharp, jagged lines look far more dangerous. When drawing evil characters, such as Terrible Tony and Sinister Sydney here, emphasize strong facial structures, hard cheekbones, and severe expressions to make them look like lean and hungry scoundrels.

◀ HEROES
Heroes in cartoons are usually conventionally attractive, with square jaws and strong cheekbones. A spiky haircut, a streak of white through a head of black hair, or a dramatic eyepatch can add individuality and hint at a darker side.

◀ SOFT TOUCH
He may not look like he could save the world, since this kind-hearted fellow is anything but hard and heroic-looking. I drew the basic structure of the head and then filled out the lower half, obliterating the neck and leaving only a hint of a chin. Rounded curves under the eyes, full cheeks, and a simpering mouth add to the effect of softness.

19

Body Building

THE NEXT LOGICAL STEP after drawing faces is to tackle the whole darn figure. Taking a life drawing class can be very beneficial, but you can also just grab your sketchbook and park yourself on a park bench. Knock out quick sketches of kids playing, yuppies jogging, and dogwalkers dogwalking. Freewheeling *gesture drawings* (see below) done in a few seconds are a great way to get a feel for poses and anatomy. Good skills in drawing the human figure accurately will give you an excellent base from which to abstract and caricature.

Artist's Tip
If you want a model who never gets tired, buy a poseable wooden mannequin at an art supply store.

▶ **HEADS UP**
The human body is measured in heads for artistic purposes. The ideal form is about 8 heads high. Cartoonists and fashion illustrators exaggerate this proportion frequently. Superheroes, monsters, and evil mutants are often 9 or more heads tall, giving them a massive, imposing appearance.

Move It

Quick gesture drawings give you a sense of how the body moves in space. Start with a stick figure. This is the cartoon's skeleton, and it defines the pose and general proportions. The backbone is the line of action determining the stance and energy the figure will have. Remember that a backbone is flexible, and so is your pencil line. Depending on the curve you give, the figure can seem rigid with attention, curving and willowy, or drooping with exhaustion. Flesh it out with rounded shapes to suggest a large chest and small hips. Then reverse it, drawing the same stick figure, but with a small chest and large hips. Quite a change, huh? Better skip the candy bar today.

◀ **SIMPLY A MATTER OF BALANCE** Your cartoon character may be out of whack, but to make it look convincing in action, its pose should be balanced.

Working out the pose in a series of gesture drawings first will help you create stances that don't put your 'toon in danger of toppling over.

Building Blocks

The best way to do anything complicated is to divide the job into simpler stages. To build a house, you start with the foundation, then add the walls and roof. You wouldn't start with the roof and work your way down to the ground. To ensure that your finished drawing is not out of proportion (unless you want it to be), here are four simple stages you can use to create an illustrated cartoon character.

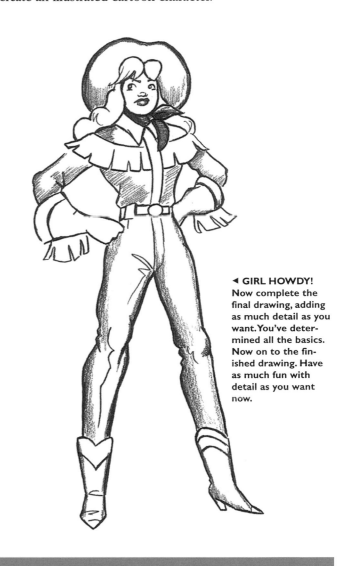

▲ STEP RIGHT UP
Start out with your stick figure skeleton to get the basic pose and proportions. Think about the tilt and perspective of the body and head.

▲ TAKING SHAPE
Add rounded shapes to indicate the body mass, hips, chest, arms, and legs. Decide whether your character is thin, fat, or muscular.

▲ RANCH DRESSING
Rough in the hands, hair, features, and costume; then smooth out your lines.

◄ GIRL HOWDY!
Now complete the final drawing, adding as much detail as you want. You've determined all the basics. Now on to the finished drawing. Have as much fun with detail as you want now.

► PLAY AGAINST TYPE Superheroes are usually tall and heroic, but who's to say you can't create a hero who is short and slight? If so, pointed ears, a skintight space suit, and a flashy mask may be *de rigueur*. But what if your ideal hero turns out to be a mild-mannered cartoonist whose markers are really magic and whose power pencils can draw an escape hatch in a chamber of doom, or... Sorry, I got carried away.

Handy Tips

Hands can be a challenge. For realistic 'toons, you'll need to show all ten fingers, so practice now. (Try drawing the hands below.) Steel fists, feeble fingers, plump palms, gnarled knuckles—each hand here has a unique personality depending on which aspects are emphasized.

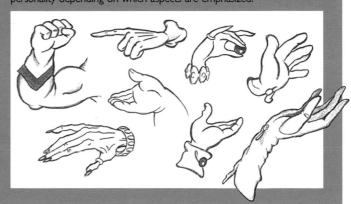

Realistic Rover

THE DOGS, CATS, LIONS, TIGERS, and bears in illustrated cartoons must be rendered in a style consistent with their human counterparts, and they must be able to convey emotions. This is another area where photographic references will come in handy. The goal is to create the impression of muscles, bone, feathers, and fur realistic enough to be believable, yet streamlined into cartoon shorthand. Facial features need to be humanized so they can then be exaggerated for effect. The emotions they express should be clear enough to leave no doubt whether they are bewitched, bothered, or merely bewildered.

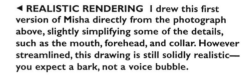

◄ MY HERO
This portrait of a German Shepherd is very germane—to the issue of humanization. Strong, noble features and an intelligent look make this guy a good candidate for a canine champion.

◄ REALISTIC RENDERING I drew this first version of Misha directly from the photograph above, slightly simplifying some of the details, such as the mouth, forehead, and collar. However streamlined, this drawing is still solidly realistic—you expect a bark, not a voice bubble.

Start with the Head

Cartoon animals can be designed to combine anatomy and stylized expressions. Instead of a construction of simple shapes, try to suggest the underlying muscles and bones. Proportions are exaggerated, but they are grounded in reality. Photographic references can be helpful here as well. Start with a realistic representation, and then simplify the animal, emphasizing its actions and expressions. Then let your creative juices loose: the photo should be a guide and inspiration, not a straightjacket.

► SEEING SPOTS
Here Misha has been turned into a "realistic" cartoon, but she is far more cartoon than real. The structure of the body and the pattern of the fur have been stylized, and, in typical cartoon fashion, her face and feet have been enlarged for an easy "read." She's definitely still a dog, but her happy smile is distinctly human.

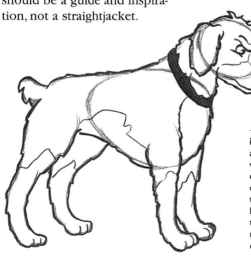

◄ REALITY BITES If it weren't for the eyes and the nose, this would be a realistic drawing. The stare is decidedly cartoonish, though. Start with a large egg shape for the body to get the right width for the chest and rib cage.

◄ GOING TO TOWN
We've gone one more step away from the photo, altering the position and shape of the ear, enlarging the nose, bugging out the eyes, and rubberizing the limbs. Although she is recognizable as a Dalmatian, Misha has become a full-fledged zany.

▶ **TALL STORY** As with the Dalmatian, the eyes and ears of this wistful giraffe are larger, and his facial expression is far more human than you'd see on the real McCoy. His hooves have also been enlarged, and the design of his coat simplified. Yet the result seems quite believably natural.

▶ **KITTY CORNER** The tabby at right was drawn in a simplified but fairly straightforward way. She's just an ordinary cat—period. The fat cat below right is a tad cartoonier, with his cranky nature reflected by his angry smirk. The slinky, seated cat above has been slenderized and elongated—but her demeanor is still pure feline. Her arched brow and sly grin suggest a sophisticated city slicker.

◀ **CAT TALES** One moment purr-fectly charming and the next rapaciously predatory, cats of all sizes have complex personalities that make them versatile actors in cartoons. They can be lovable pets or zanies, and their mysterious qualities make them well suited as heavies as well. The happy, household tabby, the hissing witch's sidekick, and the sinuous jungle denizen have all been immortalized in cartoons.

▶ **WILD THINGS** Jungle cats, such as this lioness, look a lot like their domesticated cousins, but they are more muscular and—with their powerful heads and large jaws—far more imposing. I followed the same procedure with these big cats: simplifying the shapes and emphasizing and enlarging the facial features.

Dress 'Em Up

AS A CARTOONIST, YOU ARE not only the casting director and author of your cartoons but the costume designer as well. Clothes make the man, as the saying goes, and you can get a lot of mileage out of the duds you choose for your "brainchildren."

Add Some Definition

Costume is very important in defining a character. For instance, pin a star on a hound and he's instantly perceived as a law dog. Add a cowboy hat and you've got a sheriff. Or draw a circle around the same hound's head to serve as a space helmet, and scatter a few stars in the background and Rover's in orbit! Play up aspects of dress that make it clear what kind of person this is at a glance.

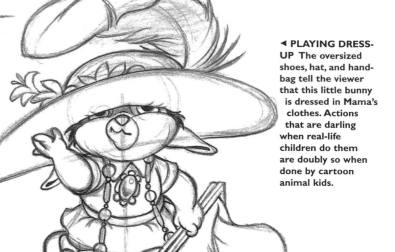

◀ **PLAYING DRESS-UP** The oversized shoes, hat, and handbag tell the viewer that this little bunny is dressed in Mama's clothes. Actions that are darling when real-life children do them are doubly so when done by cartoon animal kids.

▶ **KIDS WILL BE KIDS** Using big props on little kids is a surefire way to elicit the "Aww . . . isn't that cute" response.

Easy Does It

Since you may have to draw the same character over and over, you need to keep the wardrobe fairly simple. Bib jeans, baseball caps, penny loafers, high-top sneakers, or a hair ribbon are simple elements that can give your characters individuality. Pockets, zippers, and buttons may be necessary in real life, but not in a cartoon.

Artist's Tip
When creating characters for comic strips or cartoons, avoid detailed patterns (such as plaids) because they're too hard to draw more than once.

▶ **QUITE A CREW** These characters started out as round-headed figures with pear-shaped bodies. Their clothing design and little details such as teeth and nails came later. Remember, the basic anatomy is your first priority: You have to have the tree before you can trim it.

Put a Lid on It

If the cartoon character wears a hat, make it a funny one or a meaningful one—or both. Obviously, a football helmet, baseball cap, or chef's hat will identify your character's occupation or activity. But in a more subtle way, a playful propeller beanie, a weather-beaten ten-gallon hat, or a fur-lined cap give you distinct clues to a cartoon's personality.

Cowboy

Hunting

Straw

Beanie

Ten-gallon

Derby

The Clothes Make the Cartoon

Remember that you are communicating visually. Your audience should understand your character's personality without reading a word. Certain articles of clothing can be very telling. A scientist's lab coat, a movie star's mink stole, a rebel's leather jacket, or a spy's trenchcoat each help identify your players and tell your story.

▶ THINK "STEREOTYPE" This guy's Hawaiian shirt instantly pegs him as a typical tourist. Baggy Bermuda shorts revealing pencil-thin legs plus colossal feet corralled in beach sandals accentuate his obnoxious aura.

Wardrobe!

A change of apparel can totally alter your perception of a character. Here, our lady chameleon has been given four distinct changes of costume, makeup, and coiffure, radically altering her personality. Try this exercise on a cartoon of your own design.

IN BUSINESS You can just bet that our plain Jane here is wearing a pair of sensible shoes.

IN MOVIES Peek-a-boo hair and some white mink give starlet Jayne some real Hollywood glamour.

IN OUTER SPACE A space-age suit and gravity-defying hair make Jupiter Jane ready for blast-off.

IN "DE NILE" A serpentine head-dress and a little eyeliner turn plain Jane into a veritable Cleopatra.

Talking Toasters and Trees

AN ANIMATED CARTOON MAY FEATURE props such as an old sputtering jalopy, an obnoxious alarm clock, or a whistling teakettle brimming with personality. The props in your cartoons can also become players in the plot. For example, a steam engine may smoke, rattle, and jump around like a bucking bronco—and still be just a train in cartoon terms. Sometimes an object becomes enchanted, or simply develops a life of its own. As a result, a magic lamp might display a face, a voice, and the ability to move, truly becoming a character in the story—and, occasionally, the hero.

Household Hints

Telephones, mustard jars, radios, dishwashers, and other household objects can be drawn with lots of bounce and style. As with human characters—exaggerate and simplify! Too much detail bores the viewer and makes the picture needlessly complicated. You may choose to forget about adding limbs and hands when giving personality to inanimate objects. You can play off of what's there already, allowing table legs to dance or the cord of an appliance to become as agile as a monkey's tail.

▶ BRANCH OUT
This sour apple tree's bark is worse than its bite. Tree branches often look like noses, arms, and fingers. The knotholes and lumps in tree bark can suggest cheeks, eyes, and mouths. Why not see what kind of personality you can craft for a weeping willow or a quaking aspen?

▲ HI-JACK A jack-o-lantern is sort of an outlandish subject to start with, making it great fun to cartoon.

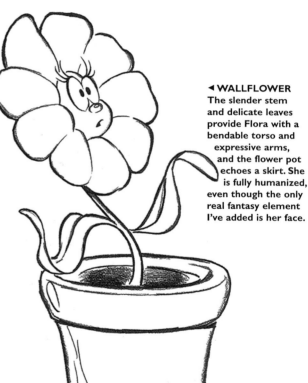

◀ WALLFLOWER
The slender stem and delicate leaves provide Flora with a bendable torso and expressive arms, and the flower pot echoes a skirt. She is fully humanized, even though the only real fantasy element I've added is her face.

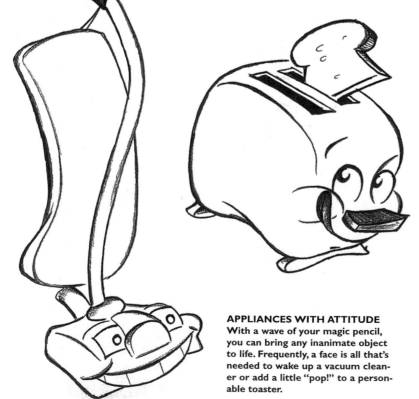

APPLIANCES WITH ATTITUDE
With a wave of your magic pencil, you can bring any inanimate object to life. Frequently, a face is all that's needed to wake up a vacuum cleaner or add a little "pop!" to a personable toaster.

◀ PICK A PERSONALITY
French-roasted coffee has gone to this percolator's head, and he now wears his lid as a jaunty beret. It's fun to play off the personalities that different objects suggest. For example, does the sugar bowl have a sweet tooth? Or does the pepper mill make the salt shaker sneeze?

On the Go

IF CARTOON ANIMALS CAN ACT LIKE PEOPLE, why not create cartoon vehicles that do so as well? Cars, boats, planes, and trains are popular characters in cartoons and children's books. They are colorful, have fun shapes, and have the ability to move around, giving the illusion of life. In addition, headlights, bumpers, and propellers often make them look as though they have faces. It's up to you to accentuate these features and turn your propeller plane into a pal.

Car-Toons

A grumbling old pickup truck? A jaunty jalopy? A sultry sports car? What personalities do the vehicles you see everyday suggest to you? The hard metal skin of an auto becomes soft and supple in a cartoon. Think of the vehicles you draw as being made out of very soft, pliable rubber rather than of steel.

PLANES ...
Vintage sports cars, small planes, and tugboats are kind of round and puffy in the first place—perfect for cute and cuddly cartoon characters. Emphasize these aspects with softly curving lines. The front windows of this little jet easily translate into a pair of eyes. The biplane's propellers make a natural nose, and its wings and wheels suggest arms and legs.

TRAINS ...
Puffs of smoke get smaller as they fade into the distance, making this happy little engine appear to chug toward you.

...AND AUTOMOBILES
A car is made up of hundreds of parts, but you don't need to doodle all of them. Here only the elements that define the identity and amplify the personality of the spunky hot rod above and silky sports car below are used. Edit out as many extra details as possible. Remember, simplify, simplify, simplify!

Location, Location, Location

WHEN YOU DRAW CARTOONS, you are creating not just characters, but the whole world they live in as well. Chairs, street lamps, cuckoo clocks, convertibles, and fire hydrants are just a few of the props that pop up periodically. The artist designs props to heighten the mood and strengthen the story line of his cartoon. The choice of which props to use depends on whether it's a jungle saga or a big-city crime drama, whether it takes place in the future or the Stone Age, and whether or not it's intended to amuse, thrill, or chill.

▶ **HOT WHEELS** Cars can be long, lean limos or brawny RVs. This sporty little car has been stripped of distracting details. Maybe you'd like to do a little additional customizing. Hey, you're the boss.

◀ **PICTURE THIS** Just a few details in the background are often enough to pin down a locale. An oriental rug on the floor or a picture on the wall can flesh out an interior. Does your scene require a homey still life or something in a gilded frame?

▼ **HOUSING PROJECT** Even houses can be designed to have a whimsical cartoon personality. Softening the lines of the roof and walls accentuate the warmth of this country cottage.

▶ **IN THE DOGHOUSE** A water bowl and bone help Prince feel his doghouse is his castle. The individual boards of the roof suggest the architect was a 10-year-old.

ACCESSORIZE Subtle or not-so-subtle distortion adds personality to mundane objects. The fat forms of this dripping faucet accentuate its humor. This alarming clock stretches and squashes as it clangs away.

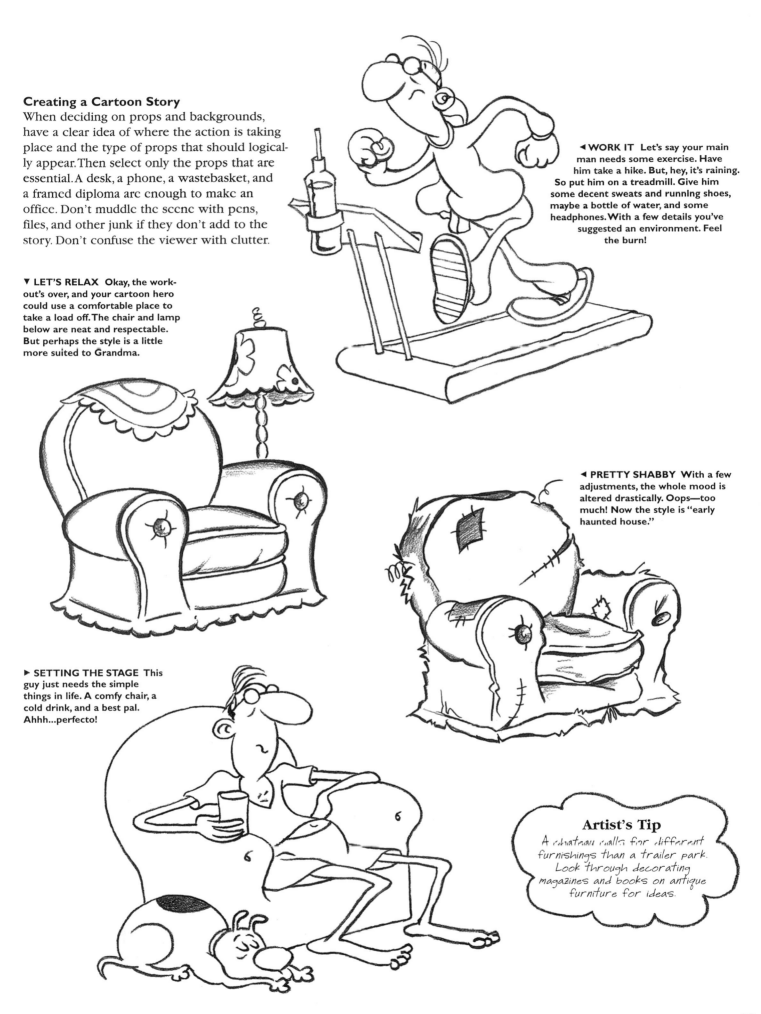

Creating a Cartoon Story

When deciding on props and backgrounds, have a clear idea of where the action is taking place and the type of props that should logically appear. Then select only the props that are essential. A desk, a phone, a wastebasket, and a framed diploma are enough to make an office. Don't muddle the scene with pens, files, and other junk if they don't add to the story. Don't confuse the viewer with clutter.

◄ **WORK IT** Let's say your main man needs some exercise. Have him take a hike. But, hey, it's raining. So put him on a treadmill. Give him some decent sweats and running shoes, maybe a bottle of water, and some headphones. With a few details you've suggested an environment. Feel the burn!

▼ **LET'S RELAX** Okay, the workout's over, and your cartoon hero could use a comfortable place to take a load off. The chair and lamp below are neat and respectable. But perhaps the style is a little more suited to Grandma.

◄ **PRETTY SHABBY** With a few adjustments, the whole mood is altered drastically. Oops—too much! Now the style is "early haunted house."

► **SETTING THE STAGE** This guy just needs the simple things in life. A comfy chair, a cold drink, and a best pal. Ahhh...perfecto!

Artist's Tip
A chateau calls for different furnishings than a trailer park. Look through decorating magazines and books on antique furniture for ideas.

Creating a Model Sheet

WHEN YOU HAVE A CHARACTER you really like and plan to draw a lot, put together a model sheet like the one shown here. A model sheet is a group of drawings of a character in a variety of poses and expressions and from a bunch of different angles. This is where cartoonists pin down the details of body construction and costume, as well as the facial expressions that reveal the intended personality. This will help you (and your team of assistants) keep your character consistent from one drawing to the next.

▼ MODEL CITIZEN
When developing a model sheet of your original character, try to include all of its different poses and expressions—walking and talking, twisting and turning, winking and blinking. Remember, you are the creator, so you get to make all the decisions. Have fun with it!

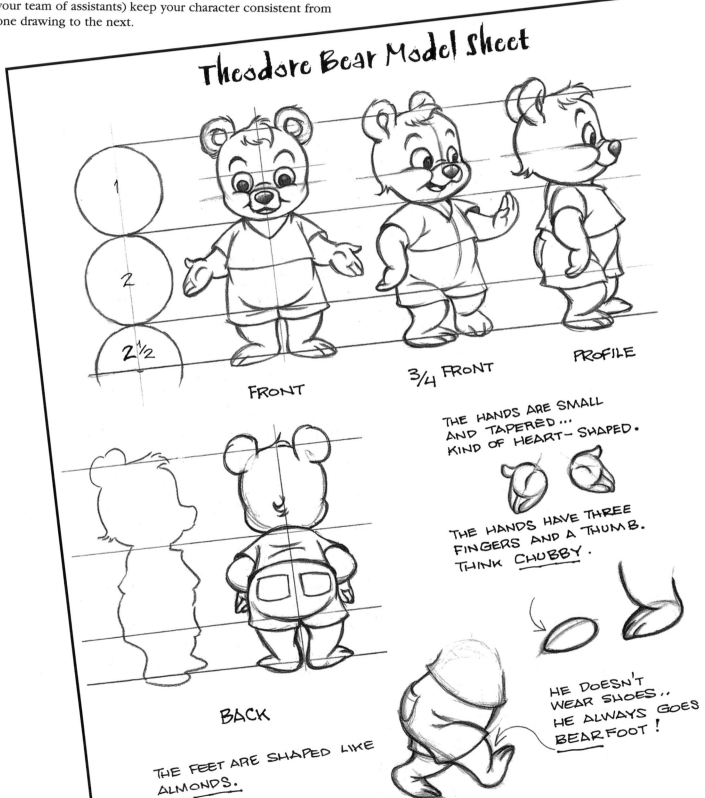

Theodore Bear Model Sheet

1

2

2½

FRONT

3/4 FRONT

PROFILE

THE HANDS ARE SMALL AND TAPERED... KIND OF HEART-SHAPED.

THE HANDS HAVE THREE FINGERS AND A THUMB. THINK CHUBBY.

BACK

THE FEET ARE SHAPED LIKE ALMONDS.

HE DOESN'T WEAR SHOES... HE ALWAYS GOES BEAR FOOT!

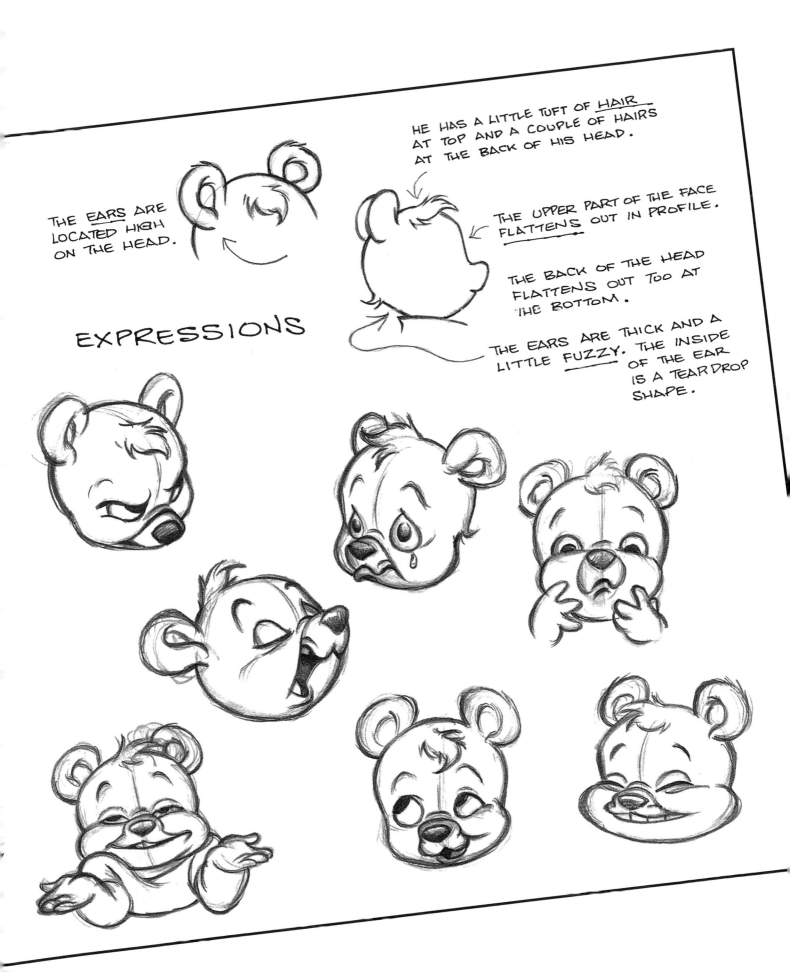

THE EARS ARE LOCATED HIGH ON THE HEAD.

HE HAS A LITTLE TUFT OF HAIR AT TOP AND A COUPLE OF HAIRS AT THE BACK OF HIS HEAD.

THE UPPER PART OF THE FACE FLATTENS OUT IN PROFILE.

THE BACK OF THE HEAD FLATTENS OUT TOO AT THE BOTTOM.

THE EARS ARE THICK AND A LITTLE FUZZY. THE INSIDE OF THE EAR IS A TEARDROP SHAPE.

EXPRESSIONS

About the Artist

Jack Keely grew up in Binghamton, New York, where his interest in illustration and art began at a young age. He spent much of his childhood drawing from comic books and inventing his own characters. He credits his parents for encouraging and cultivating his skills and talents. Jack went on to obtain his B.S.A. in illustration at the Rhode Island School of Design and his M.F.A. in design at the Cranbrook Academy of Art. To share his knowledge with others, Jack taught at North Carolina State University's School of Design and Ohio University. He also worked as an advertising art director for six years. In 1994, he moved to Los Angeles to concentrate on freelance illustration. In addition to illustrating more than 20 popular children's books, Jack has been commissioned to create artwork for magazine articles, book covers, greeting cards, and shopping bags. His cartoon characters have been translated into plush toys, plastic figures, puppets, and rubber stamps. Jack currently resides in Los Angeles.